I0435314

Contents Page

Paper Abstract

For a number of reasons, the Arctic region is seeing an increase in maritime activity and there is significant potential for that increase to continue in the future. While the present U.S. military role in the Arctic is limited, strategic and operational level leaders within the U.S. have recognized, that as Arctic activity increases, so too will the requirement for a U.S. military presence in the Arctic. The military does not currently have the capabilities which will be needed to conduct sustained operations in the Arctic. The author has identified several capability gaps which would limit the military's ability to sustain operations in the Arctic. While long term solutions do exist, they would require substantial economic commitments by the U.S. Government. Considering todays financial realities, these commitments are considered by many as unfeasible. Mitigation strategies do exist; however, through the capabilities which our international partners, interagency, and industry possess. By leveraging such capabilities, stakeholders could build the capacity through a sharing of resources and knowledge to meet the challenges that the sustainment of Arctic operations presents. This paper proposes, that by institutionalizing these relationships within a Joint Interagency Task Force North concept, the U.S. would establish a standing organization focused on Arctic military issues and a means of meeting the requirements as they emerge.

Introduction

The Arctic is changing. There has been a significant increase in maritime traffic in the region over the past ten years due to research, economic development, tourism, and access. While most experts believe that armed conflict in the Arctic is unlikely in the future, the U.S. military must be prepared to operate where others are already operating.[1] Whether for search and rescue (SAR), humanitarian assistance and disaster relief (HADR), or Maritime Domain Awareness (MDA), to successfully conduct any mission, a force must be sustained. Within the U.S. military, current or projected near future capabilities are not sufficient to sustain expected peacetime operations in the Arctic. In order to mitigate this capability gap, the military must leverage multi-national, interagency, and industry resources through a Joint Interagency Task Force North concept.

Maritime Traffic is Increasing

The Arctic is warming at twice the rate of the rest of the earth.[2] Though there is no indication that this trend will continue, the fact remains that recent higher temperatures in the Arctic have a direct effect on human activity today. As the Arctic air gets warmer, sea ice melts.[3] In addition to sea ice retreat, the ice that remains is thinning.[4] While maritime

---

[1] The Departments of Defense and Homeland Security have been tasked with a strategic level mission in the Arctic. In January of 2009, President Bush issued his Arctic Region Policy through the National Security Presidential Directive 66 and Homeland Security Presidential Directive 25 (NSPD-66/HSPD-25). The NSPD-66/HSPD-25 states that it is U.S. policy to "Meet national security and homeland security needs relevant to the Arctic region," and that "Human activity in the Arctic region is increasing and is projected to increase further in coming years. This requires the United States to assert a more active and influential national presence to protect its Arctic interests and to project sea power throughout the region." The White House, *National Security Presidential Directive 66 and Homeland Security Presidential Directive 25*, 2009 (Washington, DC: The White House, January 2009), p 1. Accessed at http://www.fas.org/irp/offdocs/nspd/nspd-66 htm

[2] David W. Titley, Courtney C. St. John, "Arctic Security Considerations and the U.S. Navy's Roadmap for the Arctic," *Naval War College Review* 63 no. 2 (2010): 36

[3] From 2001 through 2011, average sea ice has decreased 15-20% from the average in the period between 1979 through 2000. Andrey Proshutinsky, "Sea Ice and Ocean Summary," NOAA Arctic Report Card: Update 2011, last modified November 9, 2011, http://www.arctic.noaa.gov/reportcard/sea_ice_ocean.html

1

Norwegian Seas and to a lesser extent in the Bering Sea.[7] Warming conditions have had a similar effect on the cruise ship industry.

A more adventurous population, advanced ship technology and increased access have led to a growth in Arctic tourism. Since 2008, both cruise and ferry ship activity in the Arctic has increased 11%.[8] The Canadian Joint Task Force North J2 notes increases in eco-tourism and expects that in 2011, nine cruise ships will enter the Northwest Passage and into Canadian Arctic waters.[9]

Perhaps the most significant source of current growth and potential for future growth of Arctic activity is natural resource extraction. A 2008 study by the U.S. Geological Survey estimates that within the Arctic Circle[10], vast oil and natural gas reserves exist.[11] The report goes on to note that much of the oil and natural gas is assessed to be beneath the waters north of Alaska. This indicates that much of the future resource extraction may be done in or near the U.S. Economic Exclusion Zone.[12] Given these substantial reserves of natural resources, activity in the Arctic for the purpose of exploration and extraction is likely to increase.

---

[7] "Increase attributable mostly to ships remaining active in the region longer each year: average days of activity per ship increased from 68.8 in 2008 to 92.1 in 2009" Zachary D. Hamilla, "Arctic Maritime Activity Overview and Trends" (Office of Naval Intelligence brief presented at the Naval War College Fleet Arctic Operations Game, Newport, RI, September 13, 2011).

[8] Ibid.

[9] "The number of arrivals of cruise ships in Greenland ports has increased by an average of 48,9 % per year from 2005 to 2008," and between 2001 and 2008 the average rate of passengers arriving in Longyearbyen, Norway, has been growing at 14% per year. Joint Task Force (North) J2, "Expected Arctic Shipping Activity 2011" (brief provided to the Naval War College War Gaming Department, Newport, RI, June, 2011).

[10] The Arctic Circle is defined as the area north of latitude 66°33' north. Fairbanks Alaska, Arctic Circle, accessed 25 April, 2012, http://fairbanks-alaska.com/arctic-circle.htm

[11] USGS Circum-Arctic Resource Appraisal: Estimates of Undiscovered Oil and Gas North of the Arctic Circle. "90 billion barrels of oil, 1,669 trillion cubic feet of natural gas, and 44 billion barrels of natural gas liquids may remain to be found in the Arctic, of which approximately 84 percent is expected to occur in offshore areas" and that over 400 onshore oil and gas fields within the Russian, Alaskan, and Canadian Arctic contain "almost 10 percent of the world's known conventional petroleum resources." Kenneth J. Bird et al., USGS, July 23, 2008, Circum-Arctic resource appraisal; estimates of undiscovered oil and gas north of the Arctic Circle: U.S. Geological Survey Fact Sheet 2008-3049, http://pubs.usgs.gov/fs/2008/3049/.

[12] The "United States established an exclusive economic zone, the outer limit of which is a line drawn in such a manner that each point on it is 200 nautical miles from the baseline from which the breadth of the territorial sea is measured." USEEZ: Boundaries of the Exclusive Economic Zones of the United States and

Figure 2. The Arctic Circle.[13]

The Mission in the Arctic

An increase of Arctic traffic brings with it many of the missions that our military

conducts in other oceans of the world. The threat of conflict and to U.S. sovereignty in the

Arctic remains low, but as human presence grows, so too will the need to conduct SAR,

HADR in the form of oil spill response, and MDA near or within the Arctic Circle.

territories, USGS, accessed May 3, 2012,
http://coastalmap marine.usgs.gov/GISdata/basemaps/boundaries/eez/NOAA/useez_noaa.htm.
    13 www.nsf.gov

On May 12th, 2011, the U.S. Secretary of State Hillary Clinton, along with leaders from the seven other members of the Arctic Counsel, Canada, Denmark, Finland, Iceland, Norway, the Russian Federation, and Sweden, signed the Arctic Search and Rescue Agreement. It assigned regions of responsibility for each country and requires that each "shall promote the establishment, operation and maintenance of an adequate and effective search and rescue capability within its area."[14] This agreement, along with recent incidents[15], highlights the significance in addressing the SAR mission in the Arctic.

Despite the increase in accessibility, the Arctic remains a hazardous place to operate ships. As Rear Admiral Titley and Courtney C. St. John point out, "Antiquated nautical charts, drifting ice, low visibility, and the paucity of electronic and visual navigation aids hinder safety of navigation."[16] These factors, coupled with the desire for cruise ship captains to allow their passengers better views of polar bears and icebergs, for shipping companies to move their cargo on ever shorter and time saving routes, and for oil and gas companies to explore potential mines farther and farther north, will create an increased possibility of SAR missions which the U.S. will need to respond to in the near future.

Search and rescue is not the only mission that an increase in maritime traffic and human presence brings. As shipping, oil and gas exploration, and drilling becomes more prevalent, so too will the need to provide assistance for or take the lead in oil spill response

---

[14] Arctic Council, "Agreement on Cooperation on Aeronautical and Maritime Search and Rescue in the Arctic," Norsk Polarinstitutt, accessed 20 April, 2012, http://arctic-council.npolar.no/accms/export/sites/default/en/meetings/2011-nuuk-ministerial/docs/Arctic_SAR_Agreement_EN_FINAL_for_signature_21-Apr-2011.pdf.

[15] In August of 2010, the cruise ship Clipper Adventurer ran aground off Canada's Nunavut coast with 128 passengers and 69 crew members onboard. It took two days for a Canadian Coast Guard icebreaker to reach the vessel and to bring all onboard to safety. As more people seek adventure and the opportunity to observe the wildlife, geography, and natural beauty in this austere environment, so too will more of these incidents occur. Transportation Safety Board of Canada, Marine Reports-2010-M10H0006, last modified April 26, 2012, http://www.bst-tsb.gc.ca/eng/rapports-reports/marine/2010/m10h0006/m10h0006.asp.

[16] Titley, Arctic Security Considerations, 42.

operations. The requirement for this mission could come as a result of either a ship-source oil spill, as with the Exxon Valdez tanker disaster on 1989, or a well-source spill, as with Deepwater Horizon in 2010.

If an event similar to the recent one in the Gulf of Mexico were to occur in U.S. Arctic waters, the Coast Guard would again take the military lead, but other services would be required to provide support in the form of logistics, salvage, and medical support.[17] Deepwater Horizon lasted for more than three months, and while the environment, transportation nodes, and infrastructure in the Gulf of Mexico area were relatively unchallenging, they are not so in the Arctic. In its 2011 Report to Congress on Arctic Operations and the Northwest Passage, the Office of the Undersecretary of Defense assesses that in the mission area of HADR, such as an oil spill, "This mission may require the movement of resources through the air or on the surface across great distances by forces trained and equipped for the Arctic environment."[18]

Through these examples, we see how the U.S. military has been, and could be again, required to respond to the increasing threat of an oil spill in the Arctic. But to help facilitate a timely and effective response to such a call, as with SAR, the U.S. military must conduct yet a third mission in the Arctic, MDA.

MDA is defined as "the effective understanding of anything associated with the global maritime domain that could impact the security, safety, economy or environment of

---

[17] The U.S. military played a major role in the crisis response, salvage, and cleanup efforts during both of the above mentioned disasters. The National Oil and Hazardous Substances Pollution Contingency Plan (NCP) requires that "the Federal government is required to direct all public and private response efforts for certain types of spill events," as we saw in the Gulf of Mexico in 2010, when Admiral Thad Allen was assigned as the National Incident Commander of the Unified Command for the Deepwater Horizon spill. Oil Pollution Act Overview, U.S. Environmental Protection Agency, last modified January 22, 2011, http://www.epa.gov/osweroe1/content/lawsregs/opaover.htm.

[18] U.S. Department of Defense, *Report to Congress on Arctic Operations and the Northwest Passage,* (Washington, DC: 2011), p 14. Accessed at http://www.defense.gov/pubs/pdfs/Tab_A_Arctic_Report _Public.pdf

the United States."[19] One of the essential tasks of MDA is to "persistently monitor in the global maritime domain: vessels and craft, cargo, vessel crews and passengers, and all identified areas of interest."[20] Looking at the definition and task for MDA, one can see how it supports the missions of SAR (safety) and oil spill response (environment).

As Arctic traffic increases, the area becomes a more viable "global maritime domain" that requires the attention of the U.S. military. We have identified three mission areas which are most likely to present the Department of Defense and the Department (DoD) of Homeland Security (DHS) with required action in the near future. The challenges to conducting maritime operations in the Arctic, regardless of the mission, will remain relatively constant across the entire mission spectrum.

The Challenges of the Arctic Environment

To understand the challenges that military forces face when conducting missions in the Arctic, one must look at the environment. This environment includes climate, geography, biology, and social factors which could affect human operations in the Arctic.

The Arctic remains one of the most inhospitable climates for human activity on earth.[21] The effects of weather conditions on ships and aircraft can be particularly hazardous, with storms producing high winds and waves and in conjunction with freezing temperatures, the potential for icing on both platforms.[22] Frequent fog reduces visibility as well, and in a

---

[19] National Concept of Operations for Maritime Domain Awareness (Washington, DC: 2007), p 1. Accessed at http://www.gmsa.gov/references/071213mdaconops.pdf.

[20] Ibid., 5.

[21] Average January temperatures range from −40 to +32 °F and average July temperatures range from 25 to 50 °F. Fog conditions are also frequent in the Arctic, and may become more persistent with warming temperatures. Hamilla, "Arctic Maritime Activity Overview and Trends."

[22] As ice retreats, winds blow over the relatively warmer water creating storms which are particularly violent in the U.S. Arctic waters of the Beaufort and Chukchi seas. Ed Struzik, "As Arctic Sea Ice Retreats, Storms Take Toll on the Land," *Yale Environment 360*, June 6, 2011, http://e360.yale.edu/feature/as_arctic_sea_ice_retreats_storms_take_toll_on_the_land/2412/.

region which regularly sees icebergs and ice flows, this can be an acute hazard.[23] Amplifying the challenge to visibility is the fact that for much of the winter, most of the Arctic experiences nearly 24 hours of darkness per day.

The living environment must also be considered when planning any mission into the high north. Approximately half a million indigenous people live in the Arctic today. In many areas, units conducting SAR and HADR missions may rely on these indigenous populations for expertise, protection, and a source of supply and resources.[24] It is imperative that operators understand the laws, regulations, customs, of the people there, as well as the effects that maritime operations have on the native Arctic populations.

The final environmental condition we will address with regards to the Arctic is that of space. The distance to reach Arctic waters from the U.S. coast, excluding Alaska, is extremely far. From Norfolk, VA into Baffin and the Arctic Circle is approximately 2,500 nautical miles, nearly as far as a transit from Norfolk to the Straits of Gibraltar. From San Diego to the Chukchi Sea and into the Arctic is nearly 3,000 nautical miles, nearly 1,000 miles longer than a transit from San Diego to Hawaii. Once there, the Arctic is nearly 5.5 million square miles, or roughly 1.5 times the size of the continental U.S.[25] Transit times into and within the Arctic region is further hampered by the climate conditions and ice.

---

[23] As the sea ice melts and breaks apart, and violent storms create high winds, scientists have found that sea ice drift is accelerated, making possible hazards to navigation harder to predict. Gretchen Cook-Anderson, "NASA Study Finds Rising Arctic Storm Activity Sways Sea Ice, Climate," NASA, last modified October 6, 2008, http://www.nasa.gov/topics/earth/features/arctic_storm.html.

[24] Olin Strader and Alison Weisburger, "Channeling Arctic Indigenous Peoples' Knowledge Into an Arctic Region Security Architecture," The Arctic Institute, accessed April 28, 2012, http://www.thearcticinstitute.org/2012/02/channeling-arctic-indigenous-peoples.html.

[25] Arctic: Location and Geography, Polar Discovery, accessed April 20, 2012, http://polardiscovery.whoi.edu/arctic/geography.html.

The Arctic remains a very austere and hazardous place to operate. Weather, ice, biology, and distances all contribute to the challenges any ship, aircraft, or unit will face when answering the call to conduct an Arctic mission.

The U.S. Capability Gaps

For the successful completion of any mission, the U.S. military must be able to provide sustainment for equipment and personnel.[26] The U.S. has nearly mastered this function in almost every region of the world, through land, air, and sea logistics chains. However, when looking to the Arctic and the environmental factors which occur there, challenges emerge for which there are no easy solutions.

One of the primary means for the U.S. military to transport supplies, equipment, and personnel to an area of operations has been and continues to be by sea. In the Arctic region, where air operations are severely limited by weather, distance, and lack of suitable landing areas, sustainment by the sea becomes even more critical.

Currently, the U.S. Coast Guard has only one operational polar capable icebreaker, the medium icebreaker USCGC Healy.[27] The U.S. Navy has no ice-strengthened ships "available for employment in first year ice, or even in the marginal ice zone."[28] However,

---

[26] "Sustainability creates and maintains the conditions which allow maritime forces to carry out operations at the operational level within a sea, or ocean area, the adjacent coastal area, islands, and the airspace above in order to achieve a desired end state." Walter Berbrick, Christopher Gray, Leif Bergey, *Fleet Arctic Operations Game Report 2011*, Naval War College War Gaming Department, Newport, RI, September 13-16, 2011, 15, http://www.usnwc.edu/Research---Gaming/War-Gaming/Documents/Publications/Game-Reports.aspx.

[27] The USCGC Polar Star, a heavy icebreaker, is projected to be operational by December of 2012. Ronald O'Rourke, *Coast Guard Polar Icebreaker Modernization: Background and Issues for Congress*, 2012, 2, http://www.fas.org/sgp/crs/weapons/RL34391.pdf.

[28] "The marginal ice zone (MIZ) is defined as the area where open ocean processes, including specifically ocean waves, alter significantly the dynamical properties of the sea ice cover," U.S. Department of Defense, *Report to Congress on Arctic Operations*, 8-9.

because it is difficult to determine the thickness of the ice in this zone, operations remain extremely hazardous and even icebreakers are not immune to these dangers.[29]

Areas classified as ice free (less than 10% ice) present dangers to U.S. military vessels, especially those non ice-strengthened ships of the U.S. Navy. As we discussed, high winds caused by storms can blow icebergs and thick flows of sea ice into these zones. Even in the summer months, drifting ice becomes a hazard to any ship not designed to withstand the collision with minimal ice flows.

The USCGC Healy, as the U.S. military's only operational polar icebreaker, supports numerous missions including scientific research support in the Arctic and Antarctic to include the defense of U.S. sovereignty through presence in the Arctic, defense of the U.S. EEZ north of Alaska, monitoring sea traffic in the Arctic (MDA), and "conducting other typical Coast Guard missions (such as search and rescue, law enforcement, and protection of marine resources) in Arctic waters, including U.S. territorial waters north of Alaska."[30] As requirements for Arctic missions increase, the Coast Guard's single medium icebreaker will not be capable of supporting them all.

In the areas of the Arctic region where Navy ships *are* capable of operating safely, the resupply of these vessels also presents a challenge. While the Navy has nearly perfected the art of underway replenishment (UNREP), the conditions in the Arctic make this operation difficult. High winds, low visibility, and the long distances that resupply ships must travel combine to make sustainment of ships and personnel hazardous.

---

[29] In 2008, the USCGC Healy became stuck in ice which the crew assessed as being much thinner than it actually was. U.S. Coast Guard, *Report to Congress: U.S. Coast Guard Polar Operations*, 2008, 3, http://www.uscg.mil/history/docs/2008CRSUSCGPolarOps.pdf.

[30] O'Rourke, *Coast Guard Polar Icebreaker Modernization*, 1.

Minimal icebreaking capability, the lack of ice strengthened Navy ships, the difficulties of UNREP in Arctic waters, and the extreme distances for transit all contribute to a gap in the U.S. military's ability to sustain missions in the Arctic. Without a means to transport equipment, food, fuel, and personnel from ports of embarkation in the U.S., operators conducting missions in the Arctic may be required to rely on existing infrastructure for sustainment.

In contrast to the rest of the world, the Arctic has very little infrastructure for the support of medium or large scale operations. The lack of deep-water ports, airfields, and sources of fuel or basic provisions are limited, especially in the North American Arctic. There are very few places where maintenance or medical treatment is available to ships, aircraft, or personnel.

Alaska, the only U.S. state with an Arctic border, has no deep-water ports within the Arctic Circle. The most northern facility suitable for large scale maintenance of ships and major resupply is located in Kodiak, 940 miles by air from Point Barrow, on the northern border of the state. For large ships operating within the Arctic Circle, even within the U.S. EEZ, there are few places which can provide suitable resupply of fuel and provisions or maintenance support.

While the U.S. Air Force and Coast Guard operate several airbases in Alaska, these have been significantly reduced since the end of the Cold War. While Eielson Air Force Base is the most northern of all the Air Force bases in Alaska, it still remains south of the Arctic Circle and 400 miles from the northern coast.[31]

---

[31] Janine Thibault, "Surveys and maps; geobase specialty," Eielson Air Force Base, last modified January 1, 2010, http://www.eielson.af.mil/news/story.asp?id=123186417.

East of the continental U.S., the U.S. Air Force operates the most northern U.S. military base in the world, Thule Air Base in Greenland. Thule is located over 700 miles north of the Arctic Circle and boasts a 10,000 foot runway, a deep-water port and major refueling capability.[32] Thule is quite suitable for sustaining maritime operations within Baffin Bay but has no counterpart near U.S. Arctic waters north of Alaska.

One of the most challenging factors of sustaining operations in the Arctic is refueling. There are very few places within the U.S. or Canadian Arctic regions which store enough fuel to sustain large ships. In fact, most villages within the Arctic must order their fuel for heating and vehicles several years in advance, further highlighting the challenge to logistics planners when preparing for Arctic missions.[33]

A clear understanding of the environment, such as airfield and port locations, the indigenous populations and possible areas of infrastructure and mission support, as well as weather and ice reporting could help to mitigate the current lack of existing infrastructure in the Arctic.

Because the U.S. military, excluding the Coast Guard, has operated very little in the Arctic since the end of the Cold War, there is a lack of knowledge, experience, and intelligence within the U.S. regarding Arctic operations. Many of the weather and ice prediction systems available to U.S. forces are inadequate to mitigate the risk of operating even in the ice free zones and many of the navigation charts are dated and inaccurate. Timely and accurate intelligence is critical to the ability to safely sustain U.S. operations in the Arctic.

---

[32] U.S. Department of Defense, *Report to Congress on Arctic Operations*, 23.
[33] Berbrick, *Fleet Arctic Operations Game Report*, 46.

Even within the Coast Guard, which operates frequently north of Alaska, there is a need for better weather and ice prediction systems, as evidenced by the USCGC Healy becoming stuck in ice which was thicker than the crew believed it to be. If a U.S. Navy ship were to encounter the same type of situation the results could be disastrous due to their un-strengthened hulls.

In addition to a lack of knowledge and intelligence on weather and ice events, the U.S. military has little understanding of the indigenous people who live in the Arctic. As we have learned over the past decade from our experiences in Iraq and Afghanistan, successful operations rely heavily on understanding the cultures, customs, and daily lives of the people within an area of responsibility or area of operations. This is especially true in the Arctic where experience and an understanding of the environment can be crucial to survival. The military needs to understand not only how operations affect these populations, but also how they can support sustainment to operations in the Arctic.

The capability gaps which have been identified are the U.S. military's lack of adequate surface vessels for Arctic operations, a lack of infrastructure for re-supply and support, and a lack of intelligence on the Arctic environment. These gaps all hinder the U.S. military's ability to sustain any of the missions identified as most probable in the near future. Capabilities do exist; however, which can serve to mitigate these vulnerabilities and close the gaps and they must be leveraged by the U.S. military in order to create conditions where the function of sustainability can be achieved while conducting Arctic operations.

Where Capabilities Exist

The capabilities which the U.S. military lacks can be found within our foreign military partners, inter-agency groups, and industry. While the challenges described above apply to all entities, many have developed experiences, technologies, and materials which mitigate them to at least some degree.

Many nations, including countries which do not border the Arctic or Antarctic, possess polar capable icebreakers and ice hardened ships. These are primarily used for shipping support, scientific research, and resource extraction. While the U.S., an Arctic nation, has lagged behind in this capability, many of its international partners have not.

The Canadian Coast Guard currently operates 18 icebreakers, with two of those characterized as heavy and four as medium icebreakers. Primary missions of these ships include providing support to shipping vessels, transportation of cargo and fuel to villages and military units in the north, and maintenance of Canadian Arctic sovereignty.[34]

The Russian icebreaker fleet is even more robust, boasting 75 ships, 16 of which are categorized as heavy icebreakers.[35] As with the Canadian fleet, these are mainly employed in support of shipping and maintenance of Russia's northern ports. In January of 2012, we saw how cooperation and shared capabilities can avert a disaster in the Arctic. The USCGC Healy and the Russian ice-hardened tanker Renda cut through hundreds of miles of ice and successfully delivered nearly 1.3 million gallons of fuel to Nome Alaska after ice conditions lead to the cancellation of its last scheduled barge delivery of fuel of the year.[36]

Germany, Norway, Sweden and Denmark all have at least one icebreaker capable of polar operations. Most nations who possess this capability do so in order to support

[34] Icebreaking Program, Canadian Coast Guard, last modified April 13, 2012, http://www.ccg-gcc.gc.ca/eng/CCG/Ice_Who_We_Are.

[35] Lawson W. Brigham, "Soviet Arctic Marine Transportation," Martin's Marine Engineering, accessed April 15, 2012, http://www.dieselduck net/historical/02%20articles/russian htm.

[36] Yerenth Rosen, "Workers pump fuel into ice-bound Alaska port to ease shortage," *Reuters*, January 18, 2012, http://www.reuters.com/article/2012/01/18/us-fuel-nome-alaska-idUSTRE80H20D20120118.

economic development through natural resource extraction and maritime shipping support.

For this same reason, nations develop infrastructure in Arctic regions as well.

Within the U.S., in addition to the USCGC Healy, there exists one privately owned light icebreaker which is leased by the National Science Foundation (NSF). The Nathaniel B. Palmer is owned by Edison Chouest Offshore and is used primarily for scientific research in the waters of Antarctica. This demonstrates how government agencies and private industry can partner to mitigate a capability gap.

Construction in the Arctic environment is extremely costly, time consuming, and difficult due to weather conditions, characteristics of permafrost, and the extreme distances which supplies and personnel must be transported.[37] For this reason, there are few places where significant support exists for ship maintenance and refuel, medical support, or resupply. This is especially true in the Arctic of North America. There are; however, Arctic nations that have developed infrastructure to support their economies such as Norway, Iceland, and Russia.[38]

Within the Canadian Arctic, the only deep-water sea port is located in Churchill, Manitoba, located in the Hudson Bay and over 1600 air miles from U.S. Arctic waters. The Canadian military operates several airfields within the Arctic, with the most northern being Canadian Forces Station (CFS) Alert, in Nunavut.[39]

In addition to dozens of smaller ports, Norway boasts three major ports within the Arctic Circle which are classified as medium size ports.[40] Norway's largest military air base,

---

[37] U.S. Department of Defense, *Report to Congress on Arctic Operations*, 24.

[38] Arctic Council, *Arctic Marine Shipping Assessment: Arctic Marine Infrastructure*, 2009, accessed at http://www.arctic.gov/publications/AMSA/infrastructure.pdf.

[39] CFS Alert, Radio Communications and Signals Intelligence in the Royal Canadian Navy, last modified April 27, 2012, http://jproc.ca/rrp/alert html.

[40] Norway, World Port Source, accessed April 24, 2012, http://www.worldportsource.com/ports/NOR.php.

Bodo Main Air Station, is located within the Arctic Circle and very near one of the three largest ports in the Norwegian Arctic. These ports and airfields provide valuable support to both military and civilian transit, shipping, resupply, and mission support for operations in Arctic waters.

Russia has also invested heavily in port infrastructure in the north in order to support both military as well as commercial operations. While most of these are located along Russia's northwest border, there are four deep-water ports near the Bering Strait, three of which are currently closed to foreign ships.[41] Russia has very few airfields suitable for significant operations near U.S. Arctic waters.

While infrastructure in the North American Arctic is limited compared with that in Norwegian and Russian Arctic areas, this is likely to change as economic development, fueled by reports of large natural resource reserves, increases. Oil and gas mines will require storage and berthing facilities for equipment and personnel. Deepwater ports and maintenance and refueling facilities will be required to support shipping, refuel, and repair operations. For the U.S. military, the construction of this type of infrastructure is not economically feasible; however, to oil and gas companies looking to tap into the vast resources in the Arctic, it will be a necessity.[42]

As with infrastructure, many Arctic nations invest in research, systems, and training in order to support their economies. These investments, along with experience born from frequent operations and exercises, create a base of knowledge, or intelligence, of the Arctic environment. More robust systems and information sharing between nations can only serve

---

[41] Arctic Council, *Arctic Marine Shipping Assessment*, 175.
[42] Paula Lowther, "Arctic Deep Water Port," *Alaska Business Monthly*, January 2012, http://www.akbizmag.com/Alaska-Business-Monthly/January-2012/Arctic-Deep-Water-Port/.

to enhance each nation's intelligence in the Arctic further supporting the safe and effective sustainment of Arctic operations.

Two sources of intelligence that provide for safety during operations come from aids to navigation and weather and ice forecasts. The U.S. maintains no active aids to navigation (ATON) along the Alaskan coast in U.S. Arctic waters. In contrast, Canada, Denmark, Norway, Iceland and Russia all maintain some form of ATON during at least the summer months when Arctic activity is most prevalent.[43] Weather and ice forecasts throughout most of the Arctic are provided through VHF or HF radio broadcasts. These broadcasts become less reliable; however, as vessels venture farther north and away from coastlines and weather service providers. Several countries are developing satellite technology to provide critical information to mariners. Both Russia and Canada are developing satellite systems which will provide extended coverage and higher data rate transmission to mariners and operators in the Arctic.[44]

Within the U.S., federal agencies such as the National Oceanic and Atmospheric Administration (NOAA) and National Aeronautics and Space Administration (NASA) have been collaborating for years to improve Arctic weather prediction, communications, and SAR response. In 2005, NOAA launched the NASA build NOAA-N satellite, designed to more effectively monitor weather patterns in the Arctic. This satellite was also equipped with the Search and Rescue Satellite-Aided Tracking System COPAS-SARSAT which

---

[43] Ibid., 163.

[44] IMMARSAT is effective for communications up to 80 degrees north latitude and while IRIDIUM coverage is much better, it provides for low data transfer rates. Ibid., 165.

"transmits to ground stations the location of emergency beacons from ships, aircraft and people in distress."[45]

Through partnerships with foreign nations as well as the interagency, the military can vastly improve the safety and operational reach of units conducting missions in the Arctic region by leveraging technologies and practices already in use. But these systems do not represent the only form of intelligence that is required for Arctic operations and sustainment. The U.S. military must also have a good understanding of the indigenous populations who live there to include their cultures, language, daily life and expertise.

Since 1947, the Canadian Rangers have conducted safety and security missions in the Canadian Arctic. Comprised mostly of the indigenous people from Canada's Arctic Archipelago, this sub-component of the Canadian Forces "provide patrols and detachments for employment on national-security and public-safety missions in those sparsely settled northern, coastal and isolated areas of Canada which cannot conveniently or economically be covered by other elements or components of the Canadian Forces."[46] Such programs also facilitate cooperation and capacity building between the Canadian military and the indigenous populations.

Within the U.S., the Coast Guard has also taken steps to build relationships with the people indigenous to the U.S. Arctic and recognizes that "They are an invaluable resource for providing insight into the history and ongoing changes in the Arctic environment."[47] USCG District 17 employs tribal liaisons to assist in the facilitation of Coast Guard community

---

[45] Successful Launch of NOAA-N, NASA, last modified February 24, 2009, http://www.nasa.gov/mission_pages/noaa-n/main/index html.

[46] Strader, "Channeling Arctic Indigenous Peoples."

[47] U.S. Department of Defense, *Report to Congress on Arctic Operations*, 16.

outreach programs as well as to provide "greater Coast Guard access to community knowledge, resources, and support" from within those indigenous communities.[48]

As industry in the Arctic grows, it will require close collaboration between companies and the local communities which may be affected by that growth. Shell Gas, for example, employs indigenous people from Alaska's North Slope as advisors with the goal of avoiding conflict and the negative impact that resource extraction could have on the local population.[49] This type of interaction will be crucial to industry successfully maintaining a presence in the Arctic amongst the many environmental concerns associated with such activity.

The capacity exists for the collection of data, experience, and intelligence on factors which will affect sustainment in the Arctic. While the USCG has taken steps to leverage some of this knowledge with regards to the local population, the U.S. military for the most part has not. What is now required is a means for cooperation and capability sharing between existing multi-national partners, interagency, and industry to mitigate capability gaps.

Identifying the capability gaps which limit sustainment to operations in the Arctic is relatively easy. Numerous government reports from the DoD, USCG, and U.S. Navy seem to agree that ship capabilities, infrastructure, and Arctic knowledge are among them. These reports also highlight the need for cooperation among entities that possess at least parts of all of these capabilities.

Recommendation for Leveraging Existing Capabilities

---

[48] U.S. Government Accountability Office, *Coast Guard: Efforts to Identify Arctic Requirements Are Ongoing, but More Communication about Agency Planning Efforts Would Be Beneficial*, 2010, 20, http://www.gao.gov/new.items/d10870.pdf.

[49] Working with Indigenous People, Shell, accessed April 26, 2012, 4, http://www-static.shell.com/static/innovation/downloads/arctic/working_with_indigenous_people.pdf.

While symposiums, conferences and war games foster relationships, the benefits that result can be short lived as personnel move to other billets or retire. One solution is the establishment of a standing task force which would bring together Arctic stakeholders in an organization focused on capacity building. This organization would be loosely modeled on U.S. Southern Command's Joint Interagency Task Force (JIATF) South, which combines joint, interagency, and international stakeholder's capabilities in order to achieve a mission.[50]

This proposed organization, JIATF North, would be subordinate to U.S. Northern Command and would institutionalize existing relationships as well as foster new ones, creating a network of capabilities, resources, knowledge, and experience.[51] It would serve as a source for operational planning staffs, when conducting a mission analysis, to access information and potential capabilities which may not be organic to a particular service, agency, or nation.

The JIATF North would also provide a forum for stakeholders with varying levels of experience to share best practices, lessons learned, doctrine, and training techniques and even facilities in order to ensure that those operating in the Arctic environment have all the tools necessary for mission success. This organization would facilitate technology sharing and possibly even combine efforts in the development of new technologies which would benefit stakeholders.

---

[50] JIATF-S mission statement is "JIATF South conducts interagency and international Detection & Monitoring operations, and facilitates the interdiction of illicit trafficking and other narco-terrorist threats in support of national and partner nation security," and vision is "JIATF South will be the center of excellence for all-resource fusion and employment of joint, interagency, and international capabilities to eliminate illicit trafficking posing a threat to national security and regional stability." Joint Interagency Task Force South, SOUTHCOM, accessed April 13, 2012, http://www.jiatfs.southcom.mil/index.aspx.

[51] "The United States Naval War College (NWC) in Newport, Rhode Island hosted the Fleet Arctic Operations Game (FAOG) on 13-16 September 2011. The FAOG was developed and executed under the sponsorship of Commander, Second Fleet (C2F) initially and then Commander, U.S. Fleet Forces (USFF) following the integration of the two staffs. The purpose of the FAOG was to identify gaps that limit sustained maritime operations in the Arctic and recommend DOTMLPF-P actions in order to inform United States Navy leadership." During the FAOG a common theme discussed was how to best facilitate this cooperation and a JIATF North concept was proposed. Berbrick, *Fleet Arctic Operations Game Report*, 16, 19, 55, 160.

Counter-Argument

Some would argue; however, that a JIATF North is not necessary. In their evaluation

of mission trends in the Arctic through 2040, Task Force Climate Change (TFCC) predicted

that none of the Arctic missions will rise above the level of "medium," prior to 2020, within

the "Potential Mission Requirement Ranking Criteria." The only mission reaching that level

is Regional Security Cooperation.[52] Additionally, there is no general consensus within the

scientific community with regards to the rate at which sea ice is retreating, one of the major

drivers to an increase in traffic in the Arctic. The results of prediction models designed to

forecast when we will see ice free summers range from 2013 out to 2060.[53] There is, in fact,

no indication that the warming trend in the Arctic will not reverse itself in the future. These

assessments, predictions, and uncertainties, combined with current fiscal realities within the

U.S., should make Arctic operations and investments a low priority for DoD and the U.S.

government. The potential benefits, or rewards, gained by creating a JIATF North are not

worth the effort when we look at the minimal risk which we face by continuing to conduct

operations as we currently do.

Rebuttal and Conclusion

While it is true that there is no certainty that climate change will continue, sea ice will

keep melting, or that operational requirements in the Arctic will increase, it is precisely due

to the current fiscal realities faced today that the JIATF North concept will become

---

[52] Evaluation was conducted as part of the TFCC Capabilities Based Assessment published in August 2011. The CBA is classified. This data was pulled from the TFCC Navy Arctic Update brief provided at the Fleet Arctic Operations Game in September 2011. Other missions evaluated were Preventing Conflict / Deterrence, Freedom of the Seas / Sea Control, Force Projection, Maritime Security / SAR / MDA, and HA/DR / DSCA. Maritime Security/SAR/MDA was evaluated as having a potential of Low/Medium by 2020. Evaluation criteria for Low/Medium was: "Medium to low likelihood of being conducted in the Arctic," and Medium was: "Medium likelihood of being conducted in the Arctic." Blake McBride, "Navy Arctic Update" (Task Force Climate Change brief presented at the Naval War College Fleet Arctic Operations Game, Newport, RI, September 13, 2011).

[53] Bowes, *Impact of Climate Change on Naval Operations*, 8.

necessary. This organization is not a long term solution to the gaps identified, but a tool to mitigate the hazards associated with those gaps. Long term solutions, it is true, are untenable. Icebreakers, infrastructure, communications systems and satellites require enormous economic commitments. These capabilities; however, already exist among potential stakeholders of a JIATF North. By comparison, relationships are relatively inexpensive. These relationships, if institutionalized, would provide the capacity to conduct and sustain Arctic operations until the mission requires a long term financial commitment or until the Arctic freezes over again.

Bibliography

Arctic Council, "Agreement on Cooperation on Aeronautical and Maritime Search and Rescue in the Arctic," Norsk Polarinstitutt, accessed 20 April, 2012, http://arctic-council.npolar.no/accms/export/sites/default/en/meetings/2011-nuuk-ministerial/docs/Arctic_SAR_Agreement_EN_FINAL_for_signature_21-Apr-2011.pdf.

Arctic Council. Arctic Marine Shipping Assessment: Arctic Marine Infrastructure, 2009. Accessed at http://www.arctic.gov/publications/AMSA/infrastructure.pdf.

Arctic: Location and Geography. Polar Discovery. Accessed April 20, 2012. http://polardiscovery.whoi.edu/arctic/geography.html.

Berbrick, Walter, Christopher Gray, Leif Bergey. Fleet Arctic Operations Game Report 2011. Naval War College War Gaming Department, Newport, RI, September 13-16, 2011. http://www.usnwc.edu/Research---Gaming/War-Gaming/Documents/Publications/Game-Reports.aspx.

Bird, Kenneth J., Charpentier, Ronald R., Gautier, Donald L., Houseknecht, David W., Klett, Timothy R., Pitman, Janet K., Moore, Thomas E., Schenk, Christopher J., Tennyson, Marilyn E. and Wandrey, Craig J., USGS, July 23, 2008, Circum-Arctic resource appraisal; estimates of undiscovered oil and gas north of the Arctic Circle: U.S. Geological Survey Fact Sheet 2008-3049, http://pubs.usgs.gov/fs/2008/3049/.

Bowes, Michael D., Impact of Climate Change on Naval Operations in the Arctic, (CNA: 2009). Document can be obtained through the Defense Technical Information Center at www.dtic.mil.

Brigham, Lawson W. "Soviet Arctic Marine Transportation." Martin's Marine Engineering. Accessed April 15, 2012. http://www.dieselduck.net/historical/02%20articles/russian.htm.

CFS Alert. Radio Communications and Signals Intelligence in the Royal Canadian Navy. Last modified April 27, 2012. http://jproc.ca/rrp/alert.html.

Cook-Anderson, Gretchen. "NASA Study Finds Rising Arctic Storm Activity Sways Sea Ice, Climate." NASA. Last modified October 6, 2008. http://www.nasa.gov/topics/earth/features/arctic_storm.html.

Fairbanks Alaska, Arctic Circle. Accessed 25 April, 2012. http://fairbanks-Alaska.com/arctic-circle.htm.

Hamilla, Zachary D. "Arctic Maritime Activity Overview and Trends." Office of Naval Intelligence brief presented at the Naval War College Fleet Arctic Operations Game, Newport, RI, September 13, 2011.

Icebreaking Program. Canadian Coast Guard. Last modified April 13, 2012. http://www.ccg- gcc.gc.ca/eng/CCG/Ice_Who_We_Are.

Joint Interagency Task Force South. SOUTHCOM. Accessed April 13, 2012. http://www.jiatfs.southcom.mil/index.aspx.

Joint Task Force (North) J2. "Expected Arctic Shipping Activity 2011." Brief provided to the Naval War College War Gaming Department, Newport, RI, June, 2011.

Lowther, Paula. "Arctic Deep Water Port." *Alaska Business Monthly*, January 2012. http://www.akbizmag.com/Alaska-Business-Monthly/January-2012/Arctic-Deep-Water-Port/.

McBride, Blake. "Navy Arctic Update." Task Force Climate Change brief presented at the Naval War College Fleet Arctic Operations Game, Newport, RI, September 13, 2011.

National Concept of Operations for Maritime Domain Awareness. Washington, DC: 2007. Accessed at http://www.gmsa.gov/references/071213mdaconops.pdf.

Norway. World Port Source. Accessed April 24, 2012. http://www.worldportsource.com/ports/NOR.php.

Oil Pollution Act Overview, U.S. Environmental Protection Agency, last modified January 22, 2011, http://www.epa.gov/osweroe1/content/lawsregs/opaover.htm.

O'Rourke, Ronald. Coast Guard Polar Icebreaker Modernization: Background and Issues for Congress, 2012. http://www.fas.org/sgp/crs/weapons/RL34391.pdf.

Proshutinsky, Andrey. "Sea Ice and Ocean Summary," NOAA Arctic Report Card: Update 2011. Last modified November 9, 2011.   http://www.arctic.noaa.gov /reportcard/sea_ice_ocean.html.

Rosen, Yerenth. "Workers pump fuel into ice-bound Alaska port to ease shortage." Reuters, January 18, 2012. http://www.reuters.com/article/2012/01/18/us-fuel-nome-alaska-idUSTRE80H20D20120118.

Struzik, Ed. "As Arctic Sea Ice Retreats, Storms Take Toll on the Land." Yale Environment 360, June 6, 2011. http://e360.yale.edu/feature /as_arctic_sea_ice_retreats _storms_take _toll_on_the_land/24   12/.

Strader, Olin, and Alison Weisburger. "Channeling Arctic Indigenous Peoples' Knowledge into an Arctic Region Security Architecture." The Arctic Institute. Accessed April 28, 2012. http://www.thearcticinstitute.org/2012/02/channeling-arctic-indigenous-peoples.html.

Successful Launch of NOAA-N. NASA. Last modified February 24, 2009. http://www.nasa.gov/mission_pages/noaa-n/main/index.html.

Thibault, Janine. "Surveys and maps; geobase specialty." Eielson Air Force Base. Last modified January 1, 2010. http://www.eielson.af.mil/news/story.asp?id=123186417.

Titley, David W., Courtney C. St. John, "Arctic Security Considerations and the U.S. Navy's Roadmap for the Arctic," Naval War College Review 63 no. 2 (2010): 35-46.

Transportation Safety Board of Canada, Marine Reports-2010-M10H0006. Last modified April 26, 2012. http://www.bst-tsb.gc.ca/eng/rapports- reports/marine/2010 /m10h0006/m10h0006.asp.

U.S. Coast Guard, Report to Congress: U.S. Coast Guard Polar Operations, 2008. http://www.uscg.mil/history/docs/2008CRSUSCGPolarOps.pdf.

U.S. Department of Defense, Report to Congress on Arctic Operations and the Northwest Passage.Washington, DC: 2011. Accessed at http://www.defense.gov /pubs/pdfs/Tab_A_Arctic_Report_Public.pdf.

USEEZ: Boundaries of the Exclusive Economic Zones of the United States and territories. USGS. Accessed May 3, 2012. http://coastalmap.marine.usgs.gov/GISdata /basemaps/boundaries/eez/NOAA/useez_noaa.htm.

U.S. Government Accountability Office. Coast Guard: Efforts to Identify Arctic Requirements Are Ongoing, but More Communication about Agency Planning Efforts Would Be Beneficial, 2010. http://www.gao.gov/new.items/d10870.pdf.

The White House, National Security Presidential Directive 66 and Homeland Security Presidential Directive 25, 2009. Washington, DC: The White House, January 2009. Accessed at http://www.fas.org/irp/offdocs/nspd/nspd-66.htm.

Working with Indigenous People. Shell. Accessed April 26, 2012. http://www- static.shell .com/static/innovation/downloads/arctic/working_with_indigenous_people.pdf.